Texas Declaration of Independence

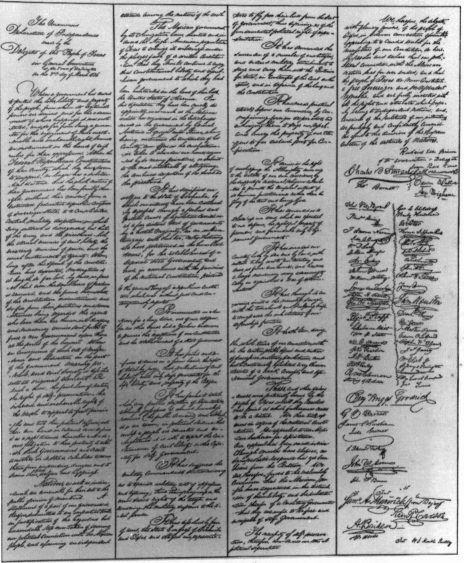

The Texas Declaration of Independence. Why didn't Austin get to sign it?

Stephen F. Austin brought 300 families to settle in Texas. They were called "The Old Three Hundred."

DID YOU EVER... MEET A TEXAS HERO?

By

Marj Gurasich

EAKIN PRESS ★ Austin, Texas

Library of Congress Cataloging-in-Publication Data

Gurasich, Marj
    Did you ever — meet a Texas hero? / by Marj Gurasich.
      p. cm.
    Includes bibliographical references.
    Summary: Provides biographies for a number of men and women important in
Texas history.
    ISBN 0-89015-819-3 : $12.95
    1. Heroes — Texas — Biography — Juvenile literature. 2. Texas — Biography
— Juvenile literature. 3. Texas — History — Juvenile literature. [1. Heroes.
    2. Texas — Biography. 3. Texas — History.] I. Title.
F385.G87   1991
976.4'00992 — dc20
[B]   91-19544
                                                       CIP
                                                         AC

Contents

Jane Long is called the "Mother of Texas." Do you know why?

Jane Long

DID YOU EVER . . . make a promise that was hard to keep?
Jane Long did.

Jane Wilkinson's father and mother died before Jane was thirteen years old. But her uncle, Gen. James Wilkinson, took care of her and gave her everything she wanted. She had pretty dresses and went to a special school. She loved parties and dancing.

One day when Jane was sixteen, her maid, Kian, ran to tell her not to go to school. Kian wanted Jane to meet a handsome doctor who was visiting in the house. Jane knew she should be in school. But she was curious. So she waited for the doctor to come down the stairs.

The minute she saw Dr. James Long, Jane

fell in love with him. He felt the same way about her. Even though Jane was so young, they decided to get married.

Uncle James did not want Jane to marry Dr. Long. But Jane found a way. In Louisiana, where they lived, a law said that orphans could choose their own guardians. Jane chose Dr. Long.

They were married in 1815. The next year they had their first child, Ann.

Besides being a doctor, James tried farming and shopkeeping. He wasn't happy with any of those jobs.

Then he heard of some trouble over land boundaries. A treaty called the Louisiana Purchase gave up any claim the United States had to the territory called Texas. James wanted to help Texas free itself from Spain. He formed an army of 300 men and left for Nacogdoches, Texas, in 1819.

Jane was very sad. She wanted to go with James, but she could not go. Her second baby would be born soon. She sewed a red and white silk flag for her husband to fly over his fort. She and little Ann kissed him goodbye.

Dr. Long went to Nacogdoches, raised Jane's flag, and said that Texas was free. But he sent some of his men to guard other places. Not enough of them stayed at the Old Stone Fort.

Two weeks after Jane's second baby, Rebecca, was born, Jane and Kian left Louisiana to join James. Jane left Ann and baby Rebecca with her sister. When they got there, Dr. Long had gone to Galveston Island to see the pirate Jean Lafitte. He hoped Lafitte would help him win freedom for Texas.

Lafitte said no to James. He had troubles of his own and could spare no money or men.

When James heard of a Spanish army marching toward Nacogdoches, he hurried back. Jane was already safely across the Sabine River in the United States. He and his men followed.

It was a sad time for Jane. She learned that her baby, Rebecca, had died in Louisiana. In those early days there were few doctors and little medicine. Many babies and children died.

When the Spanish soldiers got to Nacogdoches, it was empty. They burned the town and went back to San Antonio.

Dr. Long would not give up. He took his men to Bolivar Point, near Galveston Island. Jane and Kian met him in April of 1820.

There they learned that Jean Lafitte had been ordered by the United States Navy to leave

3

Galveston Island. He invited the Longs to have dinner with him on board his ship, *The Pride*. James would not go but told Jane to go without him. She did. *The Pride* had beautiful furniture, china, and linens. The glow from candles set in silver candlesticks shone on Jane's dark curls as she danced with Jean Lafitte after dinner. She never forgot the evening she spent with the famous buccaneer.

A few days later, Lafitte and his men burned his Galveston house and sailed away to the Yucatan Peninsula. Jane never saw him again.

The Longs went back to New Orleans to recruit more men. One of the new recruits was Ben Milam, a trader with the Indians. He and the Longs became good friends. James and his men sailed back to Bolivar Point. Jane and Kian joined him there in December.

Soon James left Bolivar Point to attack the Spanish at La Bahía (Goliad). Jane wanted to go along. James said she must remain there; her next baby was nearly due.

She promised her husband that she would wait for him until his return to Bolivar. She didn't know then how hard it would be to keep that promise.

Dr. Long and his men were captured by the Spanish army and taken to Mexico City as prisoners. He was finally freed, but a Mexican soldier shot and killed him.

Ben Milam started home to tell Jane about her husband's death, but he was captured too. He spent the next ten months in prison.

When Dr. Long left, Jane expected him back in a week or two. But the weeks dragged on . . . and on. Food at the little mud fort got very low. People were afraid to wait any longer. They came to Jane and begged her to leave with them.

She said no. She had a promise to keep.

Finally everyone left, except Jane and Kian.

It was very lonely.

While the weather was good, they fished and Jane shot small game animals. But soon it was winter, the coldest winter Galveston Island had known. The bay froze over, and all they could find to eat were oysters and frozen fish. One day Jane watched a giant bear lumber across the ice.

The days got colder and colder. The small tent did not keep the wind out. Snow and ice piled up on the tent roof. Jane was afraid the tent would fall down. Then they would have no shelter at all.

One day Jane saw Indian fires on Galveston Island. *Karankawas!* Some folks claimed these tall, fierce Indians were cannibals! They ate human flesh!

Jane shuddered. She had to do something to fool the Indians into thinking there were many people at the fort.

In a hurry she and Kian loaded the old cannon and aimed it toward the land. She knew how to fire it — and fire it she did.

Boom!

That would scare the Indians! But she needed a flag. All forts had brave flags flying. She didn't have a flag. What could she do?

Then she thought of the answer. It was so simple.

She tied her old, red flannel petticoat to the flagpole and raised it. In the wind it made a brave show. It flew for the rest of the long, hard winter that Jane and Kian had to face. The Indians left them alone.

Kian got sick. It was a very hard time for Jane Long.

Jane would soon have her baby in the cold, lonely place where she waited for her husband. She must have wondered if she would ever dance again. But she knew she must stay there, no

Cabeza de Vaca was an early Spanish explorer. He and his friends were ship-wrecked on Galveston Island. He found the same tribe of Indians that Jane Long had to face many years later.

— Illustration by Charles Shaw,
Courtesy of Roberta Christensen, author of
Pioneers of West Galveston Island

matter how hard it was. She had to keep her promise.

In December of 1821 Jane had her third daughter, Mary James. The baby is believed to be the first Anglo-American child born in Texas.

For this reason, and because she was strong and brave, and *kept her promise,* Jane Long became known as the Mother of Texas.

Jane left the island when she learned of Dr. Long's death. She lived for many more years in Texas, in the towns of Brazoria and Richmond. She rented rooms to travelers and came to know all the important people of early Texas. She gave parties and danced with all the gentlemen. It is said that Ben Milam, President Mirabeau B. Lamar, and other gentlemen wanted Jane to marry them.

She would not. She wanted no other husband than Dr. James Long, to whom she had made a promise so very long ago.

Jane Long died in 1880, at the age of eighty-two. Not long before her death she gave a party for all her friends. The music was calling her, but she knew she was too old to dance anymore. Instead she stood, holding on to the back of a chair, watching the dancers. But anyone who looked closely could see the little slippered feet tapping out the tune's beat. Jane Long was dancing one last time, even if her partner was just an old, wooden chair.

She is buried in Morton Cemetery in Richmond, Texas.

WORD LIST

boundaries — Limiting lines; borders.
provisions — Supply of food and drinks.
rhythm — Movement with a regular beat.

Jane Long's boardinghouse in Richmond, Texas. A "boardinghouse" in those days would be called a "motel" today.

In this painting, Stephen F. Austin is signing land deeds for some of his settlers.

Stephen F. Austin

*DID YOU EVER . . . do something very hard, just
because your father asked you to?
Stephen F. Austin did.*

Stephen F. Austin loved his father and admired
him. Moses Austin loved and respected his children and his wife, Maria. He had a dream for
them and for the future of Texas. But he did not
live to see that dream come true. His son, Stephen, finished what Moses had begun.

Stephen was born in Virginia in 1793. He
had a younger sister and brother. His father
wanted the best education for his children. Stephen was sent to Connecticut to attend school.
Then he went to Transylvania University for
three years. That was all the education Stephen
received. He had to go back home to help his

father in the lead mines so that the other children could go to school too.

Stephen was sixteen when he returned home. Although he worked hard and long for his father, all their businesses failed. Stephen was elected to the Missouri legislature. By the time he was twenty-seven, he had been in the House of Representatives for six years. There he learned much about government. The information would help him later on in Texas.

Of course, he never thought he would someday travel to that faraway frontier — and even, after his death, be called the "Father of Texas." Instead, he expected to stay in Missouri and, perhaps, follow his dream to study law.

His father, Moses, had other ideas. He had heard of the great land known as Texas. He thought it would be a grand thing to take some people to settle in this new land. He hurried off to Mexico to ask permission to do so. (Spain owned Mexico and Texas at this time.)

The governor told Moses Austin he could bring 300 families into Texas if they followed all the Mexican rules. Austin agreed. But before he could carry out his plan, he became very ill. He told his wife, Maria, to tell Stephen to take his place and finish the work he had begun.

When his mother told him this, Stephen knew that his own plans must wait. He had to go to Texas and lead the 300 families safely there. He must complete his father's dream.

And he did. There were many hardships along the way, but Stephen led his settlers to the fertile area between the Brazos and the Colorado rivers in the summer of 1821.

Soon after the first colonists arrived in Texas, Mexico declared its independence from Spain and a revolution began. The Mexicans defeated Spain and gained their freedom. Now Stephen had to go to Mexico to make sure the new government would allow him to keep bringing people to Texas.

The Mexican government finally gave him permission, but by now a year had gone by. He hurried back to Texas. There he found things in a muddle. The settlers were worried about their land grants. Indians attacked outlying homesteads. The crops had failed. People were confused and angry. Stephen had to work very hard to solve all these problems. But he did and things settled down again.

In 1825 he asked to bring 500 more families into Texas. Mexico granted the request. By 1831 there were more than 5,000 people in Austin's colonies. During this time Stephen F. Austin worked very, very hard. He never thought of himself, only of his people and the little colony they had formed. He grew more and more tired and worn. He hoped for the day when he could be just a plain citizen and have a little farm of his own.

But this was not to be for Stephen. People needed him and he could not say no to them.

The settlers were becoming more and more unhappy under Mexican rule. Some even hinted that they would be better off free of Mexico, to rule their own lives!

Stephen tried to tell them that they were better off as they were. They must become good Mexican citizens.

But the people still grumbled. They had a meeting and wrote a paper. They asked Stephen to take it to Mexico City to show to the government. It told of their wishes and demands. Stephen was the one to take it, they said. He got along well with the Mexican officials and would know what to say to them.

Stephen thought this was a mistake, but he went anyway. After a long, hard trip, he arrived tired and sick. On August 1, 1833, he wrote a letter to the Mexican government asking that

Texas be made an independent state in Mexico. (At that time it was part of Coahuila.)

Instead of gaining this freedom for his people, Stephen was arrested and thrown into prison. He could not speak or write to anyone. No one came to help him. His friends were afraid to say anything, for fear the Mexican government would punish Stephen more harshly. No one knew what to do.

He was not free to return to Texas until September 1835. Antonio López de Santa Anna had made himself dictator. Now Stephen believed Texas would have to fight for its freedom. It could no longer be a part of Mexico.

When he got home to San Felipe, he told his friends about the situation. They were ready to fight. They wanted to be free.

It wasn't long until the fighting started. The Texans fought the Mexicans at Gonzales over a cannon belonging to the Texans. This battle, on October 2, 1835, was the first battle of the Revolution.

At first Austin was elected commander-in-chief of the army. But things did not go well. Texas needed money in order to fight the war. Stephen was chosen to go to the United States to ask for loans and help. Sam Houston took over as commander of the army.

While Stephen was gone in search of funds for the army, the fort in San Antonio de Bexar (the Alamo) fell to the Mexicans. All the men of the Alamo died in the battle or were killed by Santa Anna afterward. Then 300 more were killed at Goliad.

Stephen F. Austin felt a great sadness come over him. He wrote, "My heart and soul are sick, but my spirit is unbroken. Texas will rise again."

Before Stephen returned home in June of 1836, Santa Anna had been defeated by Sam Houston's troops at San Jacinto. The battle on April 21, 1836, lasted only eighteen minutes.

Everyone was very happy. Texas was free! Now things would be better!

The Texas Republic had many problems to work out, and Stephen F. Austin stood by, ready to do whatever his people and Texas needed. He hoped to be its first president. But Sam Houston won that honor. He asked Stephen to become secretary of state.

Stephen was unhappy that he was not to be president, but he took the job of secretary of state and got to work.

16

He worked long and hard to help get the new republic in order. Then his health began to fail. Instead of taking care of himself he kept right on working, often in unheated rooms.

He became sick and died on December 27, 1836, barely eight months after his beloved Texas became a free republic.

He never got to have his farm, or his private life, or a family of his own. He considered as his family each and every settler who came to Texas.

And he knew that he had honored his father's last wish — that he carry on the dream that Moses Austin had begun.

And so, it seems right that grateful Texans have for generations called Stephen Fuller Austin a special name: The Father of Texas.

WORD LIST

dictator — Person who rules completely.
elect — Choose by voting.
independence — Freedom from the control of others.
land grant — Land given to person by government.
legislature — Group of persons who make laws.
revolution — Complete change in government.

Mary Austin Holly loved to write. Her book, Texas, *caused many people to come to Texas.*

Mary Austin Holley

DID YOU EVER . . . write about a trip you took?
Mary Austin Holley did.

Mary Austin Holley liked to write. She also liked to travel. When she went on trips she wrote letters to her friends and family about her adventures. She wrote in a journal every day, telling what she had done. She described the scenery and what the weather was like that day. She told about people and how they lived.

Her book about Texas was the first one published and sent everywhere so that people could read about this strange new land. It made folks want to move to Texas and start new lives. That is just what Mary Austin Holley had tried to do in her book, *Texas*.

Mary Austin was a cousin of the Father of

19

Texas, Stephen F. Austin. She was the fourth of eight children born to Elijah Austin and Esther Phelps. Her father was a shipbuilder in Connecticut. He sent one of his ships to faraway China. It returned many months later with tea and silks and beautiful things. Mary loved to hear the sea stories her father told her, and to visit the docks and see the sailing ships. *Someday,* she thought, *I will go on long voyages and see new things.* She did go on sea voyages when she grew up, but she was always very seasick!

Life was good for the Austin family until Elijah died of yellow fever in 1794. Mary was only ten years old. Because there was no money to keep such a large family, Mary was sent to live with her Uncle Timothy Phelps. His new wife, Jennett, helped make Mary happy there. Uncle Timothy sent her to a good school.

She took music lessons on her aunt's rosewood piano. She also learned to play the guitar and, in later life, took hers everywhere she went. She loved to play and sing for her friends. Although she loved music and art and dancing, her favorite subjects were always reading and writing stories and poems.

As she grew up, Mary became a pretty young woman. She liked nice clothes and wore her hair in the latest fashion. Although many young men came "courting," she chose one very special one and sent the rest away.

At the age of twenty-one, she married Horace Holley. Horace was a minister who had many friends, some of them famous men, like Thomas Jefferson.

Horace decided to go to Kentucky to become the head of Transylvania University. Later he ran a boys' school in New Orleans.

In 1827 he died of yellow fever, just as Mary's father had. He left Mary with very little money. She had two children — Harriette, who was nineteen and already married, and a son, Horace, nine years old.

Mary had to do something to support herself and her son, so she took a job teaching the children of some friends in Louisiana.

Mary's brother, Henry, had settled in Texas. Her cousin, Stephen F. Austin, put aside a large tract of land for her out of his grant from the Mexican government. At that time Texas was a part of Mexico.

Mary could not wait to visit Texas. She sailed from New Orleans in the fall of 1831 and landed at Brazoria. Her brother took her to Bolivar to his new home. There she got to know her cousin, Stephen, better. Some people say that they fell in love and planned to marry, but no one knows for sure. We do know, though, that Mary Austin Holley fell in love with Texas. Her books and diaries and letters tell us so.

She decided to write a travel book about Texas. Her book, *Texas,* was published in 1833.

When her brother's wife died, Mary took his five children to raise with her own son. They lived in Kentucky.

Mary still thought of Texas and of her cousin, Stephen F. Austin. They wrote long letters to each other. Austin told Mary that he was going to Mexico City to talk to the president about Texas. The people of Texas wanted more freedoms under Mexican law. Instead of talking, the leaders put Austin in jail. He was held prisoner in Mexico for over a year.

When he returned he told the people of Texas that they would have to fight for freedom. Mexico under the dictator Santa Anna would never give them the rights they demanded and deserved.

Mary's second book about Texas was published in 1836, but before she could return there her cousin, Stephen, died. Mary was very sad and wrote a poem in memory of the Father of

Texas, Stephen F. Austin.

On her next trip to Texas, Mary met Sam Houston and Mirabeau B. Lamar. For the next few years she spent much time in Texas, always writing about the wonders of the land and the people.

Mary died in a yellow fever epidemic in 1846, soon after Texas became the twenty-eighth state in the United States of America.

Texans should be grateful to Mary Austin Holley.

She loved to travel and she loved Texas. Mostly, she loved to write and share her thoughts with others. Her words made people want to live in the new land. Many came just because they had read one of her books.

She left her books, poetry, and songs as a lasting gift to the people of Texas.

WORD LIST

courting — Trying to win the love of someone.
diaries — Books for writing down daily happenings, thoughts, etc.
dictator — Person who rules with complete power.
journal — A daily record; same as diary.
publish — Prepare and offer a book for sale.
voyage — A journey across the ocean.

Travis liked to wear his fancy uniform and carry his sword. Did all the men at the Alamo wear uniforms?

William Barret Travis

*DID YOU EVER . . . try to write a letter that
folks would always remember?
William Barret Travis did.*

People called William Barret (Buck) Travis a
dandy. He had his clothes made by the finest tailor in town. He took frequent baths (unusual for
those days) and kept his red hair shining. He
courted all the ladies and wrote notes about
them in his diary. When he joined the army in
Texas, he had his uniforms specially made.

William Barret Travis was the eldest of ten
children. He was born on August 1, 1809, on his
father's plantation in Saluda County, South Car-
olina. By the time he was nine years old, William and his family had moved to a farm near
Sparta, Alabama. While William attended

school near his home, his father added land, cattle, and slaves to his farm.

Before he was twenty years old, Travis was already studying to become a lawyer and was also teaching school. He liked to speak in public. He liked to write things down. As a lawyer he could do both.

He married Rosanna E. Cato, a former student of his. They had two children, Charles Edward and Susan Isabella.

One day, in 1831, Travis decided to go to Texas. He got on his horse and rode away. No one knows why he left his family behind. Historians disagree about this.

Travis reached Brazoria, Texas, in May of 1831. The muddy streets and dirty shacks must have made the "dandy" turn up his nose in disgust. But he was determined to make the best of it. He signed up for a land grant and opened a law office in Anahuac.

He made some new friends. One of them was "Three-Legged Willie." R. M. Williamson had had a sickness as a boy which caused his right leg to draw up behind him. He had a wooden leg attached to his knee so that he could walk. Then he had the tailor make his pants with three legs and always wore a shoe on his useless foot. Willie loved people. He liked to tell stories, sing songs, and enjoy life. He and Travis became close friends.

Another friend was Patrick C. Jack, Travis's law partner for a time. The three men went everywhere together and were known to play jokes on each other and on anyone who got their attention.

One of their pranks got Jack and Travis arrested and thrown into prison. In order to free them, a group of 160 men marched on the fort where they were being held by an officer named Bradburn. People did not like this Bradburn because he had taken some of their freedoms from them. So they were eager to fight him and help their friends escape.

Bradburn fled for his life, and Travis and Jack were freed. Some people think that what happened in Anahuac was the real beginning of the Texas Revolution. If so, William Barret Travis was certainly an important part of that beginning.

Feelings between the Mexican government and the Texian settlers became worse and worse. Antonio López de Santa Anna became a dictator. Some of the Texas leaders thought the only answer was to declare independence from Mexico, even if it meant war!

Travis moved to San Felipe de Austin, named for its founder, Stephen F. Austin. There Travis set up his law office and met new friends. Many of them would be leaders in the revolution, when it did come, and of the new Republic of Texas. In the meantime he enjoyed the company of Austin, Ben Milam, David Burnet, and Gail Borden. He probably met Jane Long during this time.

The settlers, unhappy with the Mexican government, held several meetings at San Felipe. They sent Austin to Mexico to ask the government for better laws. Instead of meeting with Austin, the Mexicans arrested him.

Even though Travis, Houston, and many others wrote letters trying to free Austin, he was held in the Mexican prison for over a year.

People got angrier and angrier. Austin was finally freed, but the people's anger remained. Even Stephen F. Austin now said that war with Mexico was sure to come. Texans wanted their freedom!

Travis's wife got tired of waiting for him to come home. In 1836 she divorced him. He asked for his son to come live with him, and Mrs.

Travis sent the boy to Texas. Travis loved his son, Charles Edward, and was happy to see him after four years.

Travis had joined the Texas army and was ordered to San Antonio. Gen. Sam Houston, head of the army, had sent Jim Bowie to the fortress called the Alamo with orders to destroy it. Houston believed it could not be defended against the Mexican army.

But Bowie (with Travis's agreement) disobeyed Houston and, instead of destroying the fort, they hurried to make it safer and to be ready to defend it.

Jim Bowie and William Barret Travis did not like each other. Each thought he should be the leader of the troops at the Alamo. They finally agreed to share the post of commander. They would both sign all orders and have equal power.

They put the soldiers to work making the old fortress stronger. The men spent every daylight hour patching and building and putting their guns in place. They knew that war would be upon them soon.

About this time a group of "Tennessee Volunteers" came riding to the fort. They were led by the famous Davy Crockett. Travis welcomed them. Crockett entertained the men with his stories and songs.

Then Travis learned that Santa Anna was on his way. He and his many soldiers would destroy everything that got in their way. They were headed straight for San Antonio and the Alamo.

The people of San Antonio were frightened and ran away. Soon Santa Anna came and set up his camp in the city. He flew a red flag from the church spire. That meant "no quarter" — no one would be spared if the Texans did not surrender.

Travis answered the dictator by firing his big cannon toward the town square. The Texans would fight to the death.

The next day Bowie fell from a scaffold where he was trying to mount a cannon. He was badly injured and soon became feverish and very sick.

Now it was up to Travis to save the Alamo. But he gave no thought to surrender! Instead he wrote a letter to the "People of Texas and All Americans in the World."

In his letter he told of the danger they faced in the Alamo. He asked for help.

"I shall never surrender or retreat," he wrote. "I am determined to . . . die like a soldier who never forgets what is due his honor or that of his country."

He signed the letter: "VICTORY OR DEATH! William Barret Travis."

No help came. In those days, letters had to be sent by horseback. It was very hard to get the letter to San Felipe, where the leaders were meeting to set up a new Texas government. By the time it arrived there, Travis had already sent his friend Jim Bonham to seek help from Colonel Fannin at Goliad.

Again Bonham rode to Goliad, begging for help. Although he knew he faced certain death, Jim Bonham once more returned to the Alamo to help his friend, Buck Travis.

Again no help came.

Then, on March 1, help did come. From the town of Gonzales, thirty-two men marched into the Alamo.

Travis now had 182 men to defend the Alamo — against Santa Anna's thousands.

He sent out more letters. One was sent to the governor and General Houston, telling them how brave his men were in the face of such danger. He signed this letter: "God and Texas — Victory or Death."

He sent a second letter to a friend. The third

Commandancy of the Alamo—
Bejar, Feby. 24th 1836—

To the People of Texas & all Americans in the world—

Fellow citizens & compatriots—

I am besieged, by a thousand or more of the Mexicans under Santa Anna—I have sustained a continual Bombardment & cannonade for 24 hours & have not lost a man—The enemy has demanded a surrender at discretion, otherwise, the garrison are to be put to the sword, if the fort is taken—I have answered the demand with a cannon shot, & our flag still waves proudly from the walls—I shall never surrender or retreat. Then, I call on you in the name of Liberty, of patriotism & everything dear to the American character, to come to our aid,

with all despatch — The enemy is
receiving reinforcements daily &
will no doubt increase to three a
four thousand in four or five days.
If this call is neglected, I am deter
mined to sustain myself as long as
possible & die like a soldier
who never forgets what is due to
his own honor & that of his
country —

Victory or Death

William Barret Travis

Lt. Col. comdt.

P.S. The Lord is on our side —
When the enemy appeared in sight
we had not three bushels of corn —
We have since found in deserted
houses 80 or 90 bushels & got into
the walls 20 or 30 head of Beeves —

Travis

The letter written by Travis at the Alamo. What did "Victory or Death" mean?

and last was to David Ayers, the friend who was taking care of little Charles Edward.

"Take care of my little boy," the note said.

The story is told that Travis called his men together. He knew that there was no chance of any of them living through the coming battle. It is said that he took his sword and drew a line in the dirt in front of him. He told the men that they were free to go. But if they stepped across the line, that would mean that they would stay with Travis until the end.

One by one the men stepped across the line. Jim Bowie, too sick to walk, asked that his cot be carried across. Only one man, Louis Moses Rose, did not cross the line in the dust. He decided to try to escape. He climbed the wall, jumped down, and ran to freedom.

The rest of the men remained with Travis. Bowie was carried into a small room. He was armed with a gun and his famous knife. The others took their places at their guns around the fort.

When the attack came at 5:00 A.M. on March 6, the men fought bravely. Santa Anna's men were too many for them. Finally, they came over the walls. All the Texas soldiers, including William Barret Travis, James Bowie, James Bonham, and David Crockett, were killed.

Santa Anna set Mrs. Susanna Dickinson free. She was the only woman to survive the battle. He told her to take her baby, Angelina, and go tell the story of the Alamo to General Houston and to all Texians who would fight against the great Santa Anna!

But the message William Barret Travis sent out to the Texians through his letters remained in their hearts. "Remember the Alamo" would be their battle cry when they defeated the Mexicans at San Jacinto.

The handsome, red-haired dandy had earned a place in Texas history — by his written words *and* his fearless deeds.

WORD LIST

Alamo — Means "cottonwood" in Spanish; a historic Texas fort.

commander — Person who gives orders.

court — Try to win the love of.

dandy — An old-fashioned word for a young man who dressed fancy.

declare — Say; make known.

dictator — Person who rules completely.

historians — People who write about and study past times.

independence — Not under another's rule.

land grant — Land given to settlers by government.
republic — Country ruled by popular elections.
retreat — Run away.
revolution — Complete change in government.
scaffold — Temporary platform to hold workers.
surrender — Give oneself up.

The Battle of the Alamo. Did anyone live to tell what happened there?

James Bowie

DID YOU EVER . . . dream of a life of adventure?
James Bowie did.

You have to be pretty adventurous to ride an alligator. Or tame wild horses. Or fight a duel with a knife. James Bowie (everyone called him Jim) did all those things.

He lived in Kentucky from the time of his birth (1796) until his family moved to Missouri for a couple of years. Their next move was to Louisiana in 1802. It was there that Jim grew up loving adventure.

His brother Rezin wanted him to settle down, marry a nice girl, and become a farmer as he had. Jim wanted no part of that kind of life. He wanted to go to new places and find new adventures.

Bowie had many adventures. He also had some very sad times. What was the saddest thing that happened to him?

In 1828 he went to Texas, taking with him the knife his brother had designed for him. This knife would become known as the bowie knife. Jim fought several duels with it. He never went anywhere without it.

Jim was a big man. He dressed in well-tailored dark suits and polished black leather boots. He wore his hair in the latest fashion. He was a handsome, dashing fellow.

He became quite wealthy and owned great areas of land in Arkansas. When he arrived in Texas, he immediately began to deal in land and slaves. It is said that he did business with the pirate and slave trader, Jean Lafitte.

Texas was still a part of Mexico when Jim arrived there. He learned that he would have to become a Catholic and a Mexican citizen in order to buy Texas land. This he did.

Then he met and fell in love with the beautiful daughter of Lieutenant Governor Veramendi. Her name was Ursula. They were married on April 25, 1831. In a few years they had two lovely children. Jim was very happy.

Still he yearned for more adventure. He decided to search for the Lost San Saba Mines. He never found them or their treasure of silver, but sometimes people today call them the Lost

Bowie Mines. And people still search for them, just as Jim did.

Jim Bowie fought Indians and became a colonel in the Texas Rangers.

He seemed to have everything he could want in life. Then, in 1833, something happened to change his life.

His beautiful wife, Ursula, and their two children died in a cholera epidemic. Jim was very, very sad. He had loved his family very much.

Now he became more reckless than ever. He fought more Indians and didn't seem to care how much danger he faced.

When the Texians decided to fight Gen. Antonio López de Santa Anna for their freedom from Mexico, Jim Bowie was ready to help.

He fought with Ben Milam at San Antonio. Although Milam was killed in the fighting, San Antonio was freed from the Mexican army. After the battle Jim left to find more men to fight for Texas.

Jim Bowie was famous as a fighter and was liked by everyone. He soon had thirty men who wanted to go with him to fight Santa Anna.

They rode into San Antonio on January 19,

1836, and headed straight for the fortress known as the Alamo. There Jim reported to Colonel Neill that Gen. Sam Houston was ordering them to blow up and destroy the Alamo so that Santa Anna's troops could not capture it.

Jim Bowie did not agree with Sam Houston about the Alamo. Neither did Col. William B. Travis, who arrived the next day with army troops. They decided to stay at the Alamo and get ready to fight Santa Anna there.

Bowie and Travis did not get along. They could not agree on who should be the leader. Finally, they decided that they would lead the troops together. Jim would lead his volunteers and Travis would lead the army men.

This worked pretty well until Jim became very ill and could no longer lead his men. Then he turned his command over to Colonel Travis.

When Santa Anna came to San Antonio with many, many soldiers, the men in the Alamo decided to stay and fight. They knew they could not win, but they had to try. When Colonel Travis drew a line in the dust with his sword and asked anyone who wanted to stay and fight with him to cross that line, all the men (except one) stepped across. Jim was too sick to walk, but he asked the men to carry him across. He wanted to

The famous bowie knife, named for Jim, may have been designed by his brother.

stay, even if he couldn't fight in the battle.

On March 6, Santa Anna's men swarmed over the walls of the Alamo and killed all the brave men who fought there. Travis was one of the first to die. Davy Crockett and all the others died at the hands of Santa Anna's men.

Jim Bowie, too, lost his life at the Alamo. From his cot he shot his last bullet and used his bowie knife to the very end.

That was the last adventure of Jim Bowie's life. But, in dying for freedom, he probably would have said it was his best.

WORD LIST

cholera — An often fatal sickness.
citizen — A resident of a nation, state, or town.
deal — Arrangement; (v.) to buy and sell.
duel — A planned fight to settle a quarrel.
epidemic — Rapid spreading of a disease so that many people have it at once.
volunteer — Person who enters any service by choice.

David "Davy" Crockett, hero of the Alamo, wore fringed buckskins. He told tales of killing bears and Indians with his long rifle.

David Crockett

DID YOU EVER . . . tell stories and make jokes to cheer up your friends, even when you didn't feel like it?

David Crockett did.

Telling stories just seemed to "come natural" to David Crockett, called Davy by his friends and many generations of Americans.

He was born when America was still very young, in 1786. It had been only ten years since the start of the Revolution which formed a new nation of thirteen states. But David's home was not yet part of the United States. He lived in Tennessee, on the very edge of the wilderness.

When Davy was very young he did not go to school. There were no schools anywhere near where the Crocketts lived. Davy's father owned a tavern (or hotel) where Davy learned much about his world from the travelers who stopped there. They told stories, "yarns," about the far West, about Indian fights, about the big ocean far from there. Davy listened and learned from the storytellers.

One day an old Dutchman named Jacob Siler came to the tavern and noticed Davy. He thought the boy could help him on his farm in Pennsylvania. He was on his way back home and needed help with the big wagons and the horses.

Davy's father let the Dutchman take Davy with him. The boy saw new sights and learned many things from Jacob Siler. The main thing he learned was how to shoot a rifle. After much coaching and a great deal of practice, Davy became a very good shot. He liked to hunt small game to put meat on the table for himself and Mr. Siler.

Davy loved shooting the rifle, but he also missed his family. He grew very homesick. One day he couldn't stand it any longer and joined a wagon train heading back to Tennessee.

His family was glad to have him back. His father decided that it was time for Davy to attend school. A school had finally opened nearby, and Davy and his brothers enrolled.

On the fifth day of school, Davy got into a fight with the school bully. Davy won the fight, even though he was much smaller than the other boy. But he knew what the schoolmaster would do to him for fighting. Davy knew he would get a beating!

He was afraid to go back to the school. He was also afraid to tell his father what had happened. That would mean another beating. For four days he walked to school with his brothers, then hid in the woods all day until school was over.

One day the schoolmaster went to the Crockett tavern and asked Davy's father why young Davy was not in school. Was he sick?

Now Davy was in real trouble. Not only had he been in a fight, but he had lied to his father about being in school! He would really get a beating now.

He found some folks who were about to leave for Virginia. He talked them into letting him go along. But partway there he got so homesick he decided to risk the punishment and go home. Before he ever got back to Tennessee, though, he spent long months seeking adventure in Baltimore and other cities. When he finally made it back home, the fight and his punish-

47

ment were forgotten. Everyone greeted him with open arms.

By the time Davy was a young man, he had worked to pay off his father's debts, traveled about the country one way and another, and become an expert with a rifle. He could also "spin a good yarn."

He decided it was time to learn to read and write. He worked two days a week for his room and board and spent the other four days with books and slate in the little schoolhouse.

He went to school for six months. This was his only real "book larnin'."

Then David met Polly. Her real name was Mary Finley, but her Irish mother called her Polly. After a short courtship David asked Polly to become Mrs. David Crockett. Polly said yes!

The wedding was a happy one, with folks from miles around gathered at the Crockett tavern for the wedding party. There was dancing and fiddle playing and much song and laughter. It was a good start for the young couple.

Polly's mother gave them a spinning wheel, a plow, two cows, a calf, and one horse. David built a log cabin, and there Polly spun her yarn (real yarn, this time) and cooked over the open fire whatever game David brought home. His rifle still was his good friend.

The West and adventure kept calling to David. Several times over the years he packed up the animals and household goods, Polly and their three children, and moved farther west.

Until 1813. In that year the United States was at war with Britain. Many Indian tribes helped the British fight against the Americans who had come and taken away their lands.

One tribe, the Creeks, became especially angry with the settlers. The Creek people were very smart and knew many things. They were good farmers and grew cotton and tobacco. They raised chickens, cattle, horses, and sheep. They hunted elk and bear and buffalo for meat and skins.

Many of the Creeks were peaceful, but some wanted to fight. They put tall poles in their village square to show their anger. The elders, who wore red feathers in their hair, carried the poles into battle.

The settlers called these Indians "Red Sticks."

One day the Red Sticks attacked Fort Mims and many people died. The settlers were very angry. They rushed to join the militia to fight the "savages."

Polly Crockett knew that her husband would be one of the first to sign up. With tears and a deep sigh, she packed his gear and kissed him goodbye. It was the first of many such partings over the next years.

When David returned from the Creek War (as the Indian war was called), his family greeted him with a hero's welcome. He was glad to be home and vowed never to fight again.

He was nearly thirty-two years old. It was time to settle down and enjoy Polly and the children, farm his land, and grow old.

Then one day, Polly became very ill. In a few days she was dead. David could not believe it. How would he live without Polly?

He packed up and moved his household and three children, still westward.

Later he met and married a widow with two children. Elizabeth Patton was a good wife to David.

David settled down, became a magistrate (judge), and later ran for the state legislature. It was there that his ability to tell jokes and stories came in handy. He kept his audiences in laughter. He was never dull. He won the election.

After two terms he moved westward again. In western Tennessee he became known for being a bear hunter. Many of his stories in later years were about his bear hunts.

After another term in the state legislature, David ran for congressman. He was not like the other politicians hoping to go to Washington. He wore buckskin clothing and a foxskin cap, with the tail hanging down in back. He told funny stories and made people laugh. He won.

In Washington he became famous. Everyone wanted to meet the Indian and bear killer, the fellow who could tell a tall tale and make you believe it!

He was elected the second time, and many people believed he would be the next president. People liked him and knew that he was an honest man.

But one man did not like him. President Andrew Jackson and David had never liked each other. When the election came along, President Jackson and his followers defeated David for the seat in Congress.

David knew this ended his hopes to become president of the United States. He was very sad. He told his family goodbye and turned his face toward the setting sun. Time to move on.

He would go to Texas!

Once more Elizabeth packed up his clothes

and said farewell. He would send for his family, he said, as soon as he found a place in Texas.

His first stop in Texas was Nacogdoches. Then on to San Felipe de Austin. That was a place to his liking. All the most important Texans seemed to gather at the town named for Stephen F. Austin, who had brought many families to Texas. David decided to settle down there and, perhaps, once more seek office.

He learned that trouble was brewing for the colony of former Americans who had chosen this Mexican territory to make their homes. Antonio López de Santa Anna, president of Mexico, had made himself dictator. The Texians were angry and rebellious.

Never one to refuse a fight, even though he hated them, David Crockett decided to go to San Antonio. Some good men needed help there, at a place called the Alamo.

There he met Col. William B. Travis, a much younger man than the fifty-year-old Crockett. Travis and the famous Jim Bowie (whose knife made his name known all over) shared command of the fort. Bowie was very sick. The men were discouraged. Help was not coming from Fannin at the town of Goliad or from Houston at Washington-on-the-Brazos.

Crockett, as he looked when he wore "city clothes." Which way do you like him best?

Only Crockett and his seventeen "Tennesseans" had come to aid them against Santa Anna.

The dictator was leading an army of thousands toward San Antonio to overthrow the Alamo and defeat the rowdy and rebellious Texians once and for all!

David looked around at the long faces. He just couldn't help trying to cheer them up. He told bear stories and Indian stories. He sang songs and made jokes. Soon the men were chuckling and grinning. Then they were laughing out loud. They felt better. A good laugh always makes a person feel better.

But David couldn't change the outcome of the battle. For thirteen days Santa Anna and his men poured cannon fire and bullets into the fort. For thirteen days the Texians held out.

But there were too many Mexicans. They overran the walls of the Alamo and killed every one of the brave men who fought there.

David Crockett fought like a tiger to the end. He had come to Texas for a new start, a new life. That life lasted only two months. But he had chosen it so.

Even Santa Anna took note that the famous David Crockett, senator from Tennessee, was lying dead before him. But he coldly ordered that

Crockett be burned with the rest of the bodies.

David Crockett's stories and songs were stilled. But his name is remembered along with all the bravest of the men who died for liberty.

WORD LIST

bully — Someone usually larger and stronger who pushes others around.

command — To give orders.

courtship — Time of trying to win the love of someone in order to marry.

dictator — Person who rules with complete authority.

expert — Person who knows a lot about a certain thing.

game — Animals hunted for food.

generation — People born in the same time period.

militia — Army of citizens who are not regular soldiers.

rebellious — Resisting control.

slate — Chalkboard.

"spin a good yarn" — Tell a good story.

Susanna Dickinson, heroine of the Alamo. (This picture was taken many years later.) What did Santa Anna want her to do?

Susanna Dickinson

DID YOU EVER . . . have to tell someone some
very sad news?
Susanna Dickinson did.

When Susanna Dickinson was a very old
woman, people would gather around her wher-
ever she went and ask the same questions over
and over again.

"Were you really at the Battle of the
Alamo?"

"Did you really see all those brave men die?"

"Did Santa Anna really send you to tell Sam
Houston about what happened there?"

"How did Old Sam act when he heard the
sad news?"

Susanna never expected to be famous. She
was just another pioneer woman, doing all the

things a pioneer wife had to do to help put bread on her family's table.

Her family was her dear husband Almeron and her baby daughter Angelina. Their first home in Texas was in the village of Gonzales. They had moved there in 1821 from Tennessee.

She worked from sunup to sundown in her little log house. She swept the dirt floor, fed and milked the cow, cooked over an open fire, and took very good care of Angelina.

She loved her life. She loved her home and family. She was happy.

But there was trouble in Texas.

President Santa Anna had decided to become a dictator over all of Mexico. Since Texas was a part of Mexico, Santa Anna ruled Texas as well.

He would not give the people the freedoms they wanted. More and more people wanted to fight. Many signed up for the Texas army — ready to leave their farms and take their guns to fight Santa Anna.

All this made Susanna very sad. She knew Almeron would go with the others if a war should start.

There was nothing she could do but hold Angelina tightly and wait. She blinked back tears when Almeron said he had joined the Texas army.

Susanna made a serious decision.

"We are going with you," she told her husband. "We will not be left behind to worry. Angelina and I will go to San Antonio with you. We will all return to our own home someday."

Almeron grinned at her and nodded his head. They packed their belongings and started out for San Antonio.

There they stayed with friends. But one day Almeron came to tell them that Santa Anna was on his way to San Antonio. Santa Anna said he would crush the Texians. There would be a big battle, Almeron said. He was going to the Alamo fortress outside the city to help Colonel Travis and the others.

Again Susanna said, "Angelina and I are going with you!"

And again Almeron said all right.

They packed up and left their friends' home and rode to the Alamo.

It was the Battle of the Alamo on March 6, 1836, that changed Susanna's life forever.

While the men were gathering at the Alamo

fortress, other Texians were meeting to decide what to do about the freedom they so badly wanted. On March 2, 1836, they wrote a paper stating that Texas was forever free of Mexican rule. It was called the Texas Declaration of Independence.

The men at the Alamo did not know about this. In those early days of Texas there was no way to get news from one place to another except by horseback. Messengers would ride like the wind to get a letter delivered, but it still took a long time.

Everyone inside the Alamo waited for Col. William Barret Travis to tell them what to do. He and Jim Bowie were in charge of the fort. But Jim Bowie was very sick, so it was up to Travis to decide. He wrote letters, many letters, asking for help for the men inside the fort. He had only 180 men, and Santa Anna had several thousand!

Days went by and no help came.

Scouts came and said that Santa Anna was nearly there. They said that he was flying the red flag of "no quarter to the enemy." This meant that if the Alamo fell, all those inside would be killed!

Susanna shuddered. She held her baby closer to her.

For twelve days Santa Anna's men sent cannon balls over the walls of the old fort. For twelve days the men inside the fort held out. Not one man died. The Texians were hopeful that help would come.

But no help came.

On the thirteenth day, March 6, 1836, Santa Anna's soldiers broke through the walls of the Alamo. A terrible battle raged. The Texians fought as hard as they could, but there were too many Mexican soldiers. Soon nearly all the Texans were dead. Santa Anna came into the fort and ordered the rest of the Texas soldiers to be shot.

Susanna huddled in the corner of a small room. She knew her Almeron had been killed. She wondered if Santa Anna would order her killed too. Surely he would spare her baby!

A Mexican soldier came and asked Susanna her name. The *presidente,* Santa Anna, wanted to speak with her, he said. Afraid for her life and the life of Angelina, Susanna tried to hold her head high when she came before the dictator. Almeron would not have wanted her to beg for mercy.

Santa Anna surprised Susanna by telling her that she was to be spared. He offered to take her child to Mexico City and raise her in wealth and luxury. Susanna said no — never! Her child was a Texian and would remain so, no matter what!

Santa Anna shook his head. He said that, since she did not wish to accept his very generous offer, he had other plans for her.

She was to go to Gonzales. He had learned that Sam Houston, head of the Texian army, was there. He wanted Sam to get the story straight from Susanna. He wanted her to say how horrible it had been. How all the men had been killed — Colonel Travis, Jim Bowie, David Crockett, and her own husband, Almeron. He wanted her to tell General Houston how all the Texians' bodies had been burned.

Then, Santa Anna bragged, General Houston would not dare to fight the Mexican army. General Houston would give up and surrender.

He put Susanna on a horse and sent his slave, Ben, along with her for protection. Angelina rode on the horse in front of old Ben.

Tears blinded Susanna's eyes on that ride back to Gonzales. All her hopes for the future had died at the Alamo with Almeron. How could she go on?

General Houston was very kind and gentle

with Susanna. He listened as she told him the story of what had happened at the Alamo. His face grew dark with anger. He thanked her for her bravery and sent for someone to watch over her and the baby.

General Houston and his men went on to win freedom for Texas at the Battle of San Jacinto on April 21, 1836.

He must have been thinking of Susanna and all the brave men at the Alamo when he ordered his soldiers to attack Santa Anna's camp.

Leading them on his horse, he shouted, "Men, REMEMBER THE ALAMO!"

The men, following Houston into battle, yelled, "REMEMBER THE ALAMO!"

When Susanna was very old, people still asked her about the Alamo. Sometimes she had to go to court and tell the judge about a soldier and whether he really fought at the famous battle. If Susanna could remember him, she said so. Then he would receive a pension from the government.

Angelina, often called the Babe of the Alamo, died when she was only thirty-five. Susanna lived for many years in Houston. She died at the age of sixty-eight and was buried in Austin, Texas.

WORD LIST

court — Place where people accused of crimes are judged.

dictator — Person who rules with complete power.

judge — Person who hears and decides cases in a court of law.

mercy — Kindness beyond what can be expected.

pension — Money paid by the government or employer for serving over a period of time.

pioneer — Person who settles in a new part of a country.

surrender — Give oneself up.

Angelina Dickinson, Susanna's daughter, was one of several children who lived through the battle of the Alamo. Would you like to have been there?

José Antonio Navarro

*DID YOU EVER . . . suffer for something you
really believed in?
José Antonio Navarro did.*

Freedom and Texas.

José Antonio Navarro believed in both, with
all his heart.

When he was a boy, his hometown of San
Antonio, Texas, still belonged to Spain. His
father and uncle fought to win freedom for Texas
under the flag of Mexico.

Later, when Antonio López de Santa Anna
became a dictator, Navarro said that he agreed
with his good friend, Stephen F. Austin. It was
time for Texas to be free from Mexico. (Stephen
F. Austin was later called the "Father of
Texas.")

José Antonio Navarro was a peaceful man who helped his friends, Austin and Houston, make Texas great. Why was he nicknamed "The White Dove"?

José Antonio Navarro was a peaceful man. His family nicknamed him "The White Dove" because he liked to wear white suits and he always rode a white horse.

While he was still a boy his horse fell on him. His leg was badly hurt. It did not heal well. After that he always walked with a limp. He could not take up arms to fight for Texas. Instead he read many books and became a lawyer. He used his brains and skill as a lawyer to tell others that the only path for Texas was to be a *free* land.

Now the name "White Dove" fit him even better.

Navarro and his uncle, Francisco Ruiz, were the only two native Texans to sign the Texas Declaration of Independence.

At the Battle of San Jacinto, Texas won her freedom. Navarro helped write the constitution for the new Republic.

Sam Houston was the first president of the Texas Republic. He liked José Antonio Navarro and thought he was a good man.

The second president was Mirabeau B. Lamar. President Lamar did some good things for Texas. He made some laws which gave Texas its public schools.

But in 1841 he made one very bad mistake. The area west of Texas known as New Mexico wanted to become part of Texas. Lamar decided to send some men to talk to the people in Santa Fe about joining Texas.

He asked José Antonio Navarro to help lead the Santa Fe Expedition.

Navarro did not want to go, but he felt it was his duty. He loved Texas and would do anything for his homeland.

The expedition was a failure. The men got lost. They nearly starved. They had to eat some of their horses. When a few men went in search of water, Indians killed and scalped them.

After many months they finally reached Santa Fe.

The Mexican soldiers of President Santa Anna were waiting. They arrested the Texans and forced them to march to Mexico City. The trip was long and hard on the sick and weak Texans. Some died on the way. The cruel soldiers killed those who could not keep up.

Although the soldiers were mean to the Texans, the Mexican people were not. They met the prisoners with food and blankets and warm clothing. They played music and treated them as friends.

When they got to the city of Mexico, the Texans were thrown into prison. But soon many were freed and went home to Texas.

But not Navarro.

Santa Anna sent him to Vera Cruz, Mexico, to a terrible place called San Juan de Ulloa prison. He was put in a small, dark cell. The jailer locked an iron ring around his ankle. The ring had a heavy chain attached, and the chain was fastened to the stone floor of the prison cell.

It was an awful place. Navarro was very sick and unhappy there.

President Santa Anna came to visit Señor Navarro. He offered him his freedom and much money if he would stay in Mexico. But Navarro would have to tell everyone that he did not love Texas anymore.

José Antonio Navarro refused.

"I would rather die in this prison," he said, "than to give up my homeland, Texas."

He was a loyal Texan. Santa Anna called him a traitor to Mexico and kept him in the damp, dark dungeon for over three years.

But Navarro did not give in. He remained true to Texas.

Then the Mexican people revolted against

Santa Anna and put a new leader in power. José Antonio Navarro was able to escape from the prison. Some Americans helped him sneak aboard a British ship in the Vera Cruz harbor. It sailed to New Orleans, and then Navarro returned by stagecoach to Texas as a hero.

Everyone praised him for his loyalty to Texas. He was glad to get back to his family and his ranch near San Antonio.

Later, José Antonio Navarro served Texas again. When Texas became the twenty-eighth state in the United States, he helped write the state constitution.

He never stopped loving Texas.

Texas and Texans loved him too. The people named a large county for him. They even named a town in Navarro County after his father's birthplace. It was called Corsicana in honor of the Island of Corsica in Italy.

Navarro lived quietly on his ranch in his beloved Texas. When the War Between the States started, he was sad to see fighting begin again. His four sons went off to fight for the Confederacy.

The Confederate flag was the fifth of the six flags of Texas that Navarro had seen fly overhead: The Spanish flag when he was a boy. The Mexican flag until the Texas Lone Star replaced it. Then the United States Stars and Stripes when Texas became a state. Now the Confederate flag until the end of the Civil War.

Navarro lived to see his beloved Texas back in the Union, a state once more.

When José Antonio Navarro died in 1871, it is said that more people came to his funeral than San Antonio folks had ever seen before. They knew how he had suffered because he believed in Texas and freedom.

Texans will always remember The White Dove, José Antonio Navarro, and how much he loved his homeland, Texas.

WORD LIST

dictator — Person who rules completely.
dungeon — Dark, underground room to keep prisoners in.
failure — Not being able to do something.
loyal — True and faithful.
native — One who is born in a particular place.
revolt — Fight against a leader.
traitor — Person who does something against his/her country.

Sam Houston as governor of the State of Texas. Notice his leopard vest, Indian blanket, hat and cane.

Sam Houston

DID YOU EVER . . . like to dress up in funny clothes?
Sam Houston did.

It started when he was fourteen and ran away to live with the Cherokee Indians.

Sam's family was good to him. But they wanted him to do dull, boring things — like work on the farm or in the general store. When the family moved from Virginia to Tennessee, Sam was fourteen. His father was dead, but he had four bossy, older brothers. They kept him so busy, he didn't have time to read his books. If only they would leave him alone . . .

But they didn't. So Sam went off to the Tennessee River and moved in with the Cherokees. The Indians liked Sam. They called him The

Raven. The chief called Sam his son. Sam wore Indian buckskins and learned the Cherokee language. Chief Oolooteka told Sam that his special medicine animal would be the eagle. This great bird would help Sam find the right way to go in his life, the chief said.

After three years, Sam put his old store-bought clothes back on and went home. He owed some people money. So he decided to open a school. He taught until he paid back all the money he owed.

It was 1813 and America was at war with England. One day a band blared and drums rolled. A parade of soldiers marched into town. They wanted men and boys to join the army to fight the British.

Sam thought that sounded more exciting than teaching school. He enlisted.

His mother was sad to see him go. She gave him a ring to wear always. Engraved inside the ring was the word "HONOR."

Sam's first battle was against the Creek Indians. His leader was Gen. Andrew Jackson. Sam was hit in the leg by an arrow. He had a lieutenant pull out the arrow. It hurt and bled a lot. But that didn't stop him. Sam went back into the fighting anyway. He was shot again, in the shoulder and in the arm.

The doctors didn't think that Sam would live. It took a year, but he got well. By then the war was over. But General Jackson remembered young Sam Houston. And Sam remembered and loved Gen. Andrew Jackson.

Sam was disappointed the battles were over, but then the army asked him to work with the Cherokee Indians. The tribal chieftains wanted to go to Washington. The government owed them a lot of money.

Sam agreed to go with them. He put his Indian blanket around him and wound a cloth around his head as the Cherokees did.

The Indians did not get their money. Sam left the army. He did not think they had treated the Indians fairly.

He decided to become a lawyer. He studied hard. In six months he passed the test. He was a lawyer.

Now his old store clothes were gone. His Indian clothes were gone. Instead he wore clothes expected of lawyers — a fancy satin waistcoat, plum-colored coat, and a large beaver hat. He was very tall and seemed even taller with the hat on.

Sam Houston talked big talk and thought big thoughts.

In 1823 he was elected to the Congress of Tennessee. He bought a fancy new hat.

Some people liked Sam Houston. Some people hated him.

In 1827 he decided to run for governor of Tennessee. He put on a black satin vest, ruffled shirt, and Indian jacket. He even had embroidery on his socks! Then he went around the state, talking to everyone who would listen. He won.

Then Sam fell in love with Eliza Allen. She was only eighteen. Her parents wanted her to marry the new governor. Eliza wasn't sure, but she finally agreed. She and Sam were married in 1829. Three months later, Eliza left Sam and never returned. Sam refused to explain what happened.

Sam's enemies told many lies about him and his marriage. Sam decided he had to leave Tennessee. He quit his job as governor and sadly wondered what to do and where to go.

Then he saw an eagle in the sky. It swooped down over his head and flew west. He knew it was his medicine animal telling him what to do.

He went back to his Indian family. He became The Raven again. He let his hair grow long and wore it in a queue, Indian-style. He put on

Sam Houston as a young man, probably when he still lived in Tennessee. What made him run away?

Sam, dressed in his Cherokee clothes. He also sometimes wore buckskins. Who else wore these leather, fringed suits?

an Indian blanket, yellow leather leggings, and doeskin shirt. He worked hard for the Indians.

He married Tiana Rogers, the chief's niece. He built her a fine house and they ran a trading post.

When his mother died in 1831, he decided he had to make something of his life, for his mother. But he didn't know how he would do it.

He returned to Washington with an Indian delegation. One man, William Stanbery, accused Sam of being dishonest. Angry, Sam challenged Stanbery to a duel.

One night Sam strolled down the street with a friend. He saw Mr. Stanbery and set about beating him with his cane. Stanbery tried to shoot Sam, but his gun did not fire.

Sam was arrested. Before he went to court his friend, President Andrew Jackson, gave him a bag of gold coins. He ordered Sam to get some decent clothes. Sam bought a coat that reached to his knees and a handsome white satin vest.

He made a good impression on the court. He was freed. The case had brought everyone's attention back to Sam Houston. He was ready for a new life. Maybe he would move to Texas, he thought.

In 1832 he left the Cherokees, giving Tiana

his house, land, and slaves. Sadly, Tiana watched him go.

Sam headed for Texas.

He went to Nacogdoches and settled in. He dressed up in a fancy poncho and met lots of people. He was elected to go to a convention to help write a constitution for Texas in April 1833.

A man named Stephen F. Austin took a copy of this constitution and a letter to President Santa Anna in Mexico City. (Texas was part of Mexico then, under the Mexican flag.) But Santa Anna had declared himself dictator. The soldiers threw Austin in prison.

When Austin finally was released from prison in 1835, he returned to Texas. He told Sam Houston and the other Texans that they would have to fight Santa Anna to be free. There was no other way.

The loyal Texians gathered at Washington-on-the-Brazos and decided to become a republic. Sam Houston and the others signed the Declaration of Independence on March 2, 1836. He also helped work on the constitution for the new republic.

The fighting started. There were battles at Gonzales and at San Antonio. Sam Houston was made leader of the Texas army. It was a sorry, rag-tag group of untrained men. General Houston knew he needed time to train these men and recruit more.

Before he could get his troops ready for war, Santa Anna and his men had killed William Barret Travis, David Crockett, Jim Bowie, and all the other soldiers in the Alamo. A short while later, James Fannin and his men were killed at Goliad.

The people were frightened. They carried what they could, took their children, and fled toward the Sabine River and safety in the United States. They thought nothing could stop Santa Anna and his cruel men. (This was later called the Runaway Scrape.)

Sam Houston kept his men retreating, trying to gain time. People were angry at Sam and called him a coward. Why didn't he stay and fight like a man?

On April 21, 1836, Sam found the place where he would face Santa Anna. The Battle of San Jacinto took only eighteen minutes. The Texans won their victory — and their independence.

Their leader and hero, Sam Houston, had been severely wounded in his leg. He never completely recovered from this wound and walked with a limp for the rest of his life.

People returned to their homes and tried to start their lives over again. The leaders of the new republic had much work to do. They began by electing Sam Houston the first president of the Republic of Texas!

Houston worked hard, long hours trying to put the new republic together. But he liked to play too. On the first anniversary of the Battle of San Jacinto, he attended a ball in Houston City, a new town which had been named for him. Everything was just being built. No buildings had roofs or floors yet. But that didn't stop the party-goers. They hung crystal chandeliers from the bare rafters and put down a floor for dancing.

President Houston took a charming lady to the ball. His dashing outfit caused a stir among the party guests. He wore a black velvet suit, corded with gold, a bright red waistcoat, and white ruffled shirt. His boots, ankle-high, were cuffed in red leather and showed off bright silver spurs. Sam had always loved clothes!

One day he went inside a hat shop on Main Street in Houston City. He saw a hat that he just had to try on. It had a big brim, and when he put it on his head, he said, "This hat would hold ten gallons!" He bought it and wore it back to the capital. The hat store later sold 1,000 of those "ten-gallon" hats.

According to the new constitution, a president could not serve more than one term in a row. So Sam Houston had to give up the presidency after his two-year term. Mirabeau B. Lamar was elected. He and Sam did not get along. At Lamar's inauguration, Sam arrived dressed in satin knee britches and powdered wig. He looked like George Washington. Sam gave a three-hour speech. Lamar was so upset that he left. His secretary had to read his acceptance speech.

Lamar got even with Sam by moving the capital from Houston City to a place on the Colorado River nearer the center of the republic. He named it Austin after the Father of Texas, Stephen F. Austin. This made Sam very angry, and the capital was moved back and forth several times before it finally was kept in Austin.

In May of 1840, Sam married Margaret Lea. He settled down to enjoy married life — that is, until September of 1841, when he was elected president of Texas once more.

Sam's greatest hope was for Texas to become one of the United States. He worked long and hard for his dream to have Texas become part of the United States. It finally happened in December 1845. Anson Jones, then the president, lowered the Lone Star flag and Sam Houston caught it in his arms. The Stars and Stripes were raised, and Texas became the twenty-eighth state in the Union.

Once more, Sam retired. And once more, duty called. He was elected U.S. senator from the new state of Texas. Off to Washington he went, often showing up in Congress wearing a Mexican blanket and sombrero or a military cap and cloak, blue with red lining. Sam was never one to be plain!

The United States had to fight a war with Mexico over boundaries. After two years, the U.S. had won all land north of the Rio Grande River, as far west as the Pacific Ocean.

Sam ran for governor of Texas in 1857 and lost. Back in Washington, still a senator, he wore a catskin vest. He said it was leopard skin and told everyone that a leopard did not change its spots.

The next time he ran for governor, he won. He and Margaret and their seven children moved into the too-small Governor's Mansion.

Now the serious problem was the argument

between North and South about slavery. Sam believed the Union should be saved, no matter what. He believed this so much that he gave up being governor.

Tired and sad, he moved his family (they now had eight children) to Huntsville. He hoped to see the end of the tragic War Between the States. But he did not.

Sam Houston died of pneumonia on July 26, 1863.

His last words, whispered to his wife, were, "Texas . . . Texas . . . Margaret . . ."

Sam Houston may have made many people angry, but many people loved him. All remembered the man who liked to dress up in funny clothes, and who lived his life for his greatest love, Texas.

WORD LIST

anniversary — Yearly return of a special date.
chandelier — Ceiling fixture with branches for lights.
constitution — Written set of rules for a government.
convention — A meeting for a special purpose.
delegation — A group of people given power to act for others.
dictator — Person who rules with complete power.
duel — A planned fight to settle a quarrel.
elect — Choose by voting.

enlist — Join some branch of the armed services.

honor — Having special respect; dignity.

inauguration — Act of installing a person in office.

medicine animal — Some Indians believed that a special animal was given to each person to guide them through life.

queue — Braid of hair hanging down the back.

rag-tag — Sloppy.

recruit — Get people to join.

republic — Nation where leaders are elected by the people.

Sam Houston meeting his prisoner, Santa Anna, after the Battle of San Jacinto. Why is Santa Anna dressed as a farmer?

Bibliography

JANE LONG

Crawford, Ann Fears, and Crystal Sasse Ragsdale. *Women in Texas: Their Lives, Their Experiences, Their Accomplishments.* Austin, Texas: Eakin Press, 1982.

Davis, Joe Tom. *Legendary Texians, Vol. 1.* Austin, Texas: Eakin Press, 1982.

Gonzalez, Catherine Troxell. *Jane Long, The Mother of Texas.* Austin, Texas: Eakin Press, 1982.

Lamar, Mirabeau B. *Jane Long.* 1838.

Sinclair, Dorothy Tutt. *Tales of the Texians.* Bellaire, Texas: Dorothy Sinclair Enterprises, 1985.

Turner, Martha Anne. *The Life and Times of Jane Long.* Waco, Texas: Texian Press, 1969.

Wharton, Clarence R. *History of Fort Bend County.* San Antonio, Texas: The Naylor Co., 1939.

Ziegler, Jesse A. *Wave of the Gulf.* San Antonio, Texas: The Naylor Company, 1938.

STEPHEN F. AUSTIN

Allen, Edward. *Heroes of Texas.* New York: Julian Messner, 1970.

Barker, Eugene C. *The Life of Stephen F. Austin.* Austin: Texas State Historical Association, 1949.

Flynn, Jean. *Stephen F. Austin: The Father of Texas.* Burnet, Texas: Eakin Press, 1981.

Gracy, David B. II. *Moses Austin: His Life*. San Antonio: Trinity University Press, 1987.

McCall, Edith. *Stalwart Men of Early Texas*. Chicago: Children's Press, 1970.

Phegley, Mallie. *The Father of Texas: Stephen F. Austin*. San Antonio: Naylor Co., 1960.

MARY AUSTIN HOLLEY

Crawford, Ann Fears, and Crystal Sasse Ragsdale. *Women in Texas: Their Lives, Their Experiences, Their Accomplishments*. Austin, Texas: Eakin Press, 1982.

Holley, Mary Austin. *The Texas Diary, 1835–1838*. Austin, Texas: The University of Texas Press, 1965.

Lee, Rebecca Smith. *Mary Austin Holley: A Biography*. Austin, Texas: The University of Texas Press, 1962.

WILLIAM BARRET TRAVIS

Davis, Joe Tom. *Legendary Texians: Vol. I*. Austin, Texas: Eakin Press, 1982.

Flynn, Jean. *William Barret Travis*. Austin, Texas: Eakin Press, 1976.

McDonald, Archie P. *William Barrett Travis: A Biography*. Austin, Texas: Eakin Press, 1976.

Turner, Martha Anne. *William Barret Travis: His Sword and His Pen*. Waco, Texas: Texian Press, 1972.

JAMES BOWIE

Allen, Edward. *Heroes of Texas*. New York: Julian Messner, 1970.

Davis, Joe Tom. *Legendary Texians*. Austin, Texas: Eakin Press, 1982.

Flynn, Jean. *Jim Bowie, A Texas Legend*. Austin, Texas: Eakin Press, 1980.

McCall, Edith. *Stalwart Men of Early Texas*. Chicago: Children's Press, 1970.

Webb, Walter Prestcott, ed. *The Handbook of Texas*. Vol. I. Austin, Texas: Texas State Historical Association, 1952.

DAVID CROCKETT

Burke, James Wakefield. *David Crockett: The Man Behind the Myth*. Austin, Texas: Eakin Press, 1984.

Crockett, David. *A Narrative of the Life of David Crockett of the State of Tennessee*. Knoxville: The University of Tennessee Press, 1973.

Davis, Joe Tom. *Legendary Texians: Vol. I*. Austin, Texas: Eakin Press, 1982.

Townsend, Tom. *Davy Crockett: An American Hero*. Austin, Texas: Eakin Press, 1987.

SUSANNA DICKINSON

Jakes, John. *Susanna of the Alamo: A True Story*. Orlando, Florida: Harcourt Brace Jovanovich, 1986.

Kerr, Rita. *Girl of the Alamo*. Austin, Texas: Eakin Press, 1984.

King, C. Richard. *Susanna Dickinson: Messenger of the Alamo*. Austin, Texas: Shoal Creek Publishers, Inc., 1976.

JOSÉ ANTONIO NAVARRO

Barker, Eugene C. *The Life of Stephen F. Austin, Founder of Texas, 1793–1836*. Austin: The Texas State Historical Association, 1949.

Connor, Seymour V. *Adventure in Glory, The Saga of Texas: 1836–1849*. Austin, Texas: Steck-Vaughn Co., 1965.

De Cordova, J. *Texas: Her Resources and Her Public Men*. Waco, Texas: Texian Press, 1969.

Falconer, Thomas. *Letters and Notes on the Texan Santa Fe Expedition, 1841–1842*. New York: Dauber & Pine Bookshops, Inc., 1930.

Fehrenbach, T. R. *Lone Star, A History of Texas and the Texans*. New York: American Legacy Press, 1978.

Fisher, Howard T., and Marian H. Fisher, eds. *Life in Mexico — The Letters of Fanny Calderon de la Barca*. New York: Doubleday, 1966.

Gurasich, Marj. *Benito and the White Dove*. Austin, Texas: Eakin Press, 1989.

Navarro, José Antonio. *The Memoirs of José Antonio Navarro*. Translated from the original. A. Puntes Historicos.

Wharton, C. H. *The Lone Star State, A School History*. Dallas, Texas: Southern Publishing Co., 1932.

SAM HOUSTON

Bishop, Curtis Kent. *Lone Star Leader*. Englewood Cliffs, N.J.: Responsive Environments, 1961.

Fritz, Jean. *Make Way for Sam Houston*. New York: Putnam, 1986.

Gonzalez, Catherine Troxell. *Sam Houston: Hero of San Jacinto*. Austin, Texas: Eakin Press, 1983.

James, Marquis. *The Raven: A Biography of Sam Houston*. Dunwoody, Georgia: Norman S. Berg, 1929.

McCaleb, Walter. *Sam Houston*. San Antonio, Texas: Naylor, 1967.

Moyer, John William. *Famous Frontiersman*. Northbrook, Illinois: Hubbard Press, 1972.

Rickard, John Allison. *Brief Biographies of Brave Texans*. Dallas, Texas: Banks, Upshaw, 1962.